# SPECIAL EDITION:
## THE LIFE OF RAOUL

### and the Death Of
### DR. MARTIN LUTHER KING

ANTHONY G. TENNIS

*and*

GLEN R. TENNIS

PAGE PUBLISHING, INC.
New York, NY

First originally published by Page Publishing, Inc. 2019

ISBN 978-1-68456-101-8 (Paperback)
ISBN 978-1-68456-102-5 (Digital)

Printed in the United States of America

# Contents

# Preface

To the readers of this book:

In order to convince the skeptics, nonbelievers, government, and interested investigators as to the credibility of the author, Glen R. Tennis, a brief autobiography is certainly in order.

I was born on August 16, 1915, on a farm ten miles west of Kingfisher, Oklahoma, the oldest and firstborn of four sisters and one brother.

In 1921, at the age of six, our family moved to Cherokee, Oklahoma, where I went to school until November of 1925 when we moved to Clayton, New Mexico. I graduated from high school as valedictorian in 1933.

In 1938, I married and soon moved to Texas. My chosen vocation, which started in 1938, was that of an auctioneer. My own father had been one since 1921 and was a direct influence on the choice of my own career. He and I as partners were the first commercial livestock auctioneers to auction livestock in Big Spring, Texas, Sweetwater, Texas, Abilene, Texas, and San Angelo, Texas. I was the first auctioneer to sell sheep at a commercial livestock barn in San Angelo from 1938 to 1956, helping to make this city the "Wool Capital and Market of the World." From 1938 to 1956, I was the top livestock auctioneer of Texas.

From 1950 to 1957, we experienced the seven-year drought in West Texas. Due to the fact that receipts from livestock auctions were diminishing year by year, I owned, operated, and managed another type of auction. At a large building named Tennis Auction Center in

San Angelo, Texas, in which two sales per week were performed for twenty years. We sold virtually anything and everything except livestock at these sales. Due to my wife's health problems at that time, I sold my business to the current owner. After that, I owned and operated a used-wholesale establishment until 1988. I semiretired and started writing in earnest at that time.

A man lives and learns through life's experiences. I learned to be a pretty good judge of people by just being around them. During my lifetime, I came into contact with just about every type of person known to mankind. A professional psychologist could not have had a more valuable practical experience or on the job training with people with what I had. My integrity, honesty, and love for my fellow man has always been the key to success in my own life.

As you read my book, please keep in mind the fact that I am making a bold attempt to portray my opinions, beliefs, and conclusions in the most honest way possible. I will try and tell this story with no holds barred even though at times it may cast a bad light on people that I have known and loved in my life.

In the following chapters, I will expose the identity of the person that I believe James Earl Ray knew only by the name of Raoul. I will show how this man of mystery to the general public set up a common, everyday criminal as the "fall guy" for one of the most notorious assassinations that our nation has ever known.

You will come to understand the motive as well as the intense personal need that Raoul had in having Dr. Martin Luther King assassinated. You will also see how Raoul carried out this plan in such a way as to make it appear that James Earl Ray was the lone gunman.

I will show the reader how personal suspicions and gut feelings of my own drove me to investigate this event for twenty-four long years. I have finally put together this huge puzzle of dates and events between James Earl Ray and Raoul, which led to that terrible day in Memphis, Tennessee.

James Earl Ray himself would be the one to furnish the final pieces of the puzzle. After reading his own book, *Who Killed Martin Luther King? The True Story by the Alleged Assassin*, I was able to gather the information and knowledge to put the final touch on the lingering mystery.

The following chapters will reveal why the assassination committee of 1978 was as wrong as the difference between daylight and dark in their final determination that Ray acted alone and was lying about a person known only as Raoul and that individual never existed.

A shocking conspiracy between two men will also be revealed that existed in having Dr. King assassinated by using James Earl Ray as the underworld "setup" person.

This book is not being written simply for personal gain for myself or for the other people who have made this book possible. I have written this book because I believe that the possible truth concerning the assassination of Dr. Martin Luther King Jr. needs to be told to the world and believe that this truth lives within me.

# Special Notes from the Editor

A few months ago, I was offered the opportunity to help a friend edit his granddad's book. When he first told me about the substance of the book, I thought he was a crackpot. I don't think that anymore. After reading his book and James Earl Ray's book, *Who Killed Martin Luther King? The True Story by the Alleged Assassin*, I am convinced that Glen Tennis knew what he was talking about. I am also convinced that his grandson, Anthony, shares his grandfather's convictions. I carefully researched and checked the facts and references used by Glen Tennis. I made cross-references with the facts presented by James Earl Ray and FBI documents I was allowed to read. As Old Glen would have said himself, "In my horse sense way of thinking, I think it all may be true."

—J. Culp

# Synopsis of the Life of Raoul

Before presenting his brief biography, I must say that I am convinced that my stepson, James Allen Smith, was the person known by James Earl Ray as "Raoul."

He was born on July 4, 1935, at Valley View, Texas, to Mr. and Mrs. Jack Smith of that community. Jack Smith died in a WPA truck accident in 1938 and was buried at the Myra Cemetery, some ten miles west of Gainesville, Texas.

After his father's death, he was raised for a few years by his maternal grandparents, Mr. and Mrs. R. A. Wilson. He lived with them at various locations on farms near Gainesville and Valley View until the age of twelve. He came to live with us in San Angelo, Texas, when I married his mother on October 9, 1947.

His younger brother by two years continued to live with his grandparents until the summer of 1950 at which the time he came to live with us along with my two children by a former marriage. All at once, we had four teenagers to raise and send to school. To complicate matters, we adopted a three-day old baby boy in March 1952. Now the old saying became true in that "Your children and my children are beating the hell out of our children."

Soon after the death of Jack Smith, James contacted polio and spent some time at a Ft. Worth rehabilitation hospital for polio victims. There he became somewhat of a spoiled brat because of his self-pity and animosity toward his parents and grandparents. His right leg became shorter, and he walked with a slight limp. However, he would wear more than one sock in order to elevate the shorter leg and could wear the same size shoe.

At the age of twelve when he first came to live with us, he had the knowledge and actions of a sixteen-year-old. He was a very bright student in school and went one year to our local college. He became a local radio announcer and was excellent in that capacity. At that point in time, he married a divorcée with two children who lived with their father in Midland, Texas. In 1957, after one year of marriage, they were divorced due to her infidelity. However, in 1977, she revealed to us that she still loved him, and from 1958 until late April 1968, they had always been in contact with one another by letters or telephone.

After the divorce, he lost all interest in the radio business and became depressed, not knowing what to do with his life. He visited my place of business off and on for the next four years and spent a lot of time at our home just sitting around, staring and talking to himself while constantly rocking in the rocking chair. He borrowed and took money from his mother while using her car for various things. Without my knowledge, he pawned my childhood trombone, a keepsake.

I have been an auctioneer for most of my adult life. I was the first auctioneer to begin selling livestock commercially at auction barns in Texas. Auction barns opened in 1938 at Big Springs, Sweetwater, Abilene, and San Angelo, Texas. When the drought hit in the early 1950s and receipts became low; I opened, owned, and managed my own auction in San Angelo, Texas, selling everything except livestock on a two-day basis per week for the next twenty years (1955–1975).

There was one thing in particular that I remembered about James when he visited my business. It was a very distinct action on his part in regard to a customer of mine. There were certain times that he would help me load out merchandise to a man from the border town of Eagle Pass, Texas. This customer's first name was Raoul. James seemed to be very taken with this Hispanic man. He seemed to be fascinated with his name. The man's name was Raoul. James took a peculiar liking to this individual and would repeat his name, Raoul, over and over again while conversing with him. He would question the man to no end about his life and business at Eagle Pass and the town of Piedras Negras, Mexico. Most of his business came from the Mexican side of the border. I could tell that James fell in love with the name "Raoul" as he kept repeating it over and over again, at times to my embarrassment. I believed he used this name as an alias when he first met James Earl Ray in July 1967.

There was a man in San Angelo who was a steady customer of mine who was working at a paint and body shop in the early 1960s. He became a bosom friend of James and was a friend of mine.

Without my knowledge at that time, I looked back and realized that the first major crime committed by James was the stealing of a 1960 model Rambler. He had it repainted by his mutual friend who I am sure knew that it was stolen. During this period of time, James always seemed to have more than an adequate amount of cash. He refused to tell his mother or myself where it came from. He stopped residing at our house and kept to himself from then on.

I found out years later that at this point in time, he stole a new 1961 Chevrolet from a lot in Abilene and brought it to San Angelo where he parked it at night at the home of one of my employees. My employee was so scared of what he had done that when he got home that night from working at the auction, he pushed it into the Concho River. It was found when the river was dredged in the 1970s or early 1980s.

In 1962, James stole another new car and was caught while in the process of cutting it up for parts. This happened on a remote ranch at night in an abandoned building owned by an acquaintance of his younger brother.

James was sent to Huntsville state prison for two years. When he got out, he again was sent to prison from Tarrant County, Fort Worth, to Huntsville. While there, he had some dental work done. During this time, he also met his ex-wife. She was serving time for felony mail fraud extortion. They became bosom friends again and never lost contact with one another from that time on. Their whereabouts concerning each other were maintained through her contact with her mother.

When James was released from prison for the second time in 1965, he moved to Fort Worth. He married a Jewish girl from Chicago who became pregnant by him before their marriage took place. James vanished during her pregnancy. She adopted the newborn baby girl out to someone in Fort Worth and moved back to Chicago to her folks.

It was during this period of time that James went big-time stealing new cars, mostly Cadillacs and Mustangs. He had rented a building in Fort Worth where he painted and changed serial numbers to match titles that he had acquired from local junkyard dealers of totaled Caddys and Mustangs. Also at this point in time, he joined a gang of car thieves who were also stealing and hijacking big-time: jewelry, diamonds, TVs, electrical appliances, or anything else of real value. The gang's boss lived in Granbury, Texas. I learned later that James dated his daughter quite often. He became good friends with James and trusted his gangland fashion. After selling new stolen cars to outstate buyers, James would peddle stolen merchandise out of U-Haul trailers to shady buyers in West Texas.

In the spring of 1967, James had acquired a fleet of new stolen Caddys and was looking for a buyer with big money who would buy them in one package deal. He personally owned two of these Caddys, the total of which amounted to some $15,000 or so. He finally found a buyer who said they would buy all of them. My investigation revealed the prospective buyer to be Hosea Williams, head of the Southern Christian Leadership Conference (SCLC) in Atlanta, Georgia.

On a given night in the spring of 1967, the gang along with James, who were representing the sale, arrived in Atlanta to a designated warehouse where the exchange was to take place. Before the money was to be exchanged, the buyer took the titles on the pretext of seeing if they were in order. About thirty minutes later, he came back without the titles or the money. He said that they intended on keeping the cars. The public would be told that they were anonymous donations to the cause. If the gang or James did not agree with their decision, he would immediately notify the police and have them arrested for selling stolen cars. James and his gang were caught in a no-win situation. Out of fear of being arrested, they were forced to leave immediately. But not before James would make a threat that he was to fulfill in the future. Let there be no mistake about the warning and the threat that James was to fulfill in the future. Let there be no mistake about the warning and the threat that James issued to the buyer that night. If he was not paid then and there, he would kill Martin Luther King Jr. at some future date.

That night, it must have seemed like the hasty vow of a small-time con man who was desperate to be paid his money. It would not seem that way another day. James did warn and threaten the buyer that if he was not paid then and there before leaving, in the future, someway and somehow, he, James, would have Martin Luther King Jr. assassinated.

James made a vow and kept it as you will see by reading the chapters in this book. His entire fortune was wrapped up in two of these Caddys, and he wasn't about to forget it unless they were paid for. This episode haunted him day and night up and until the assassination on April 1968. After losing his fortune, he went back to Granbury to start all over again.

In July 1967, he came to San Angelo in a yellow Mustang pulling a U-Haul trailer filled with new stolen appliances. He called his mother by telephone, saying that he was passing through and did not have time to visit. This was the last time that she ever heard his voice and never saw him again. He went directly to the home of our mutual painter friend with the Mustang and U-Haul trailer. This friend lived on the outskirts of town. Later in June 1968, this man told me of James's visit with him. At the time of my discussion with this painter friend, James's corpse lay rotten on a remote ranch some six miles from Granbury.

On June 1968, after the assassination, our mutual painter friend came to me, wanting a private talk about James's visit with him. I met him at his house, and we talked privately in my pickup truck. First, he said he was a private FBI "snitch" but would never do or say anything against James due to mine and my wife's popularity and good standing as citizens.

I also stated that it is important at this point that I inform the readers that Rex Gavin died of a heart attack in 1972.

If I had not had this conversation with Rex, it would have been impossible for me to write this book. He has been the key to the whole episode. He furnished the information about my stepson's previous vow to kill Dr. King. He had supplied a motive for the assassination plan, which was in the making as early as June 1967. The conversation with Rex Gavin convinced me of James Allen Smith's involvement in the death of Dr. Martin Luther King Jr.

# My Conversation with Rex Gavin

"Did you know that James came to visit me in July of 1967?" he asked.

I said, "No, I did not, but he did telephone his mother at that time."

He paused then said, "Ever since the assassination of Martin Luther King Jr., I have been pondering and trying to make up my mind if I should tell you what I know about the visit your stepson had with me."

"Go on," I said, "I'm really interested to hear about it."

The gist of the conversation about his visit with James was as follows:

> Rex said that James drove up unexpectedly in a yellow Mustang pulling a load of stolen merchandise in a U-Haul trailer. Rex got into the car with him and noticed a two-way police radio. It could be tuned to any channel that the police might be using in any city in the USA. James said that he used it to find out if the police were looking for him, etc. He said that he always tuned it in to the police in every city he passed through. Rex knew he had been a radio announcer in San Angelo and that he was an expert at that sort of business. He

also knew that James was a thief, con man, liar, teller of unbelievable tales, joker, you name it. Half the time he didn't know whether to believe him or not. He also knew that James had served time in prison on two different occasions in the early 1960s. In their conversation, Rex asked him if he was still stealing and selling new cars or had he learned his lesson yet.

This is what he answered, knowing quite well that Rex would never "rat" on him, "I lost money on two Cadillacs that belonged to me. It happened last spring." He said, "I'm going into another line of business soon. I hope it will pay off better than stealing cars. Car stealing has become too dangerous."

Rex then asked him what he meant by losing his money. James told him the whole episode of selling the fleet of new, stolen Cadillacs and the final results.

He told Rex that a plan was in the making to have King assassinated and that it would happen! He vowed that it would happen as he was still very angry and upset about losing the two Cadillacs.

At that time, Rex thought this was another wild tale. Later after the assassination, he changed his mind. This was the reason that Rex came to me for a private talk about the whole situation. After visiting with Rex for about an hour, James left for reasons unknown. Rex never saw or heard from him again.

Rex said to me, "Do you think he really did it or had a part in it? At the time, I thought it was another one of his wild tales, but now I'm not so sure. What do you think?"

I was so flabbergasted that my guts were rolling inside of me. I remember thinking that it was all a dream and couldn't happen to his mother and me. This was something big, a national question mark, and still is to this day in time.

Rex said to me, "This has to be a conspiracy, and sooner or later, you will find the FBI was behind the whole thing. Everyone knows how Hoover hated this man. If James is involved, he had to have help from someone, and my guess is that it is Hoover and company."

After my two-hour conversation with Rex, I went on about my business but never mentioned the talk to my wife, James's mother, for fear of upsetting her to no end.

I sneaked out a large photo of James and went directly to the FBI office and reported to the man in charge. I told him Rex's story and that I thought James was involved somehow in the assassination. He said that he would look into it and report back. At this point in time, James Earl Ray was already in prison awaiting trial.

When Ray was convicted, the FBI agent called me to pick up the photograph, saying he could not find any involvement of James Allen Smith in the assassination. As I look back on this event, I can plainly see that no investigation of any importance ever took place. The reason being, in my honest opinion, that J. Edgar Hoover and company was behind the whole conspiracy.

# CHAPTER 3

# The Meeting of Raoul and James Earl Ray

As previously stated in the preface, I have read the book by James Earl Ray entitled *Who Killed Martin Luther King? The True Story by the Alleged Assassin.*

By putting the dates that James Earl Ray has furnished together with what I know about Raoul's whereabouts from early July 1967 to the day of the assassination, I will present the puzzle as I see it.

During the assassination committee's hearing on 1977 and 1978, a witness stated that a $50,000 reward would be paid by person or persons unknown for the assassination. This would be set up through a shyster attorney who would pass word of the reward through the underworld. In my opinion and logical thinking, I'm sure James Smith as "Raoul," knew about the offer at the time of the Caddy sale failure. He must have contacted Hoover during the summer of 1967 through this shyster attorney and started making plans with him for a future assassination when the time was right. As you recall, the conversation between Rex Gavin and James Smith revealed that a plan was already in the making and that the assassination would take place in the near future. This was in early July 1967. He also told Rex that he was going into a more profitable business as soon as he could unload and sell the hot merchandise in the U-Haul trailer.

In my opinion, he did just that by smuggling drugs into the United States from Canada and Nuevo Laredo, Mexico. His former

Jewish wife was from the Chicago area, and he had met her family in 1965–1966.

In my opinion, the scenario of the chance meeting of "Raoul" and Ray is as follows: After Raoul sold his stolen goods in Texas in mid-July, he immediately went to Chicago. Then he went on to Detroit and crossed into the border town of Windsor, Canada, haunting bars and taverns to gather information and make contacts for drug smuggling.

According to Ray's book, he, James Earl Ray, was hiding from the jailbreak, which occurred in Missouri. He was staying in Montreal, Canada, looking for a way to get a passport to Africa or Europe. He also needed some fast money to pay for the passport and for living expenses in the event that he did get to Africa or Europe. I drew the following conclusions from reading James Earl Ray's book about their first meeting.

The following is my own interpretation of what Ray had to say about the meeting:

> One afternoon in late July 1967, I stopped by and went into the Neptune Tavern at 121 Commerce Street in Montreal, Canada. I met an individual who seemed to be in his midthirties. He was about 5'8" or so, weigh about 140 lbs. or so, and had slightly wavy hair, dark red in color, that might have been the result of a recent hair dye. He sat down at my table, ordered a drink, and made small talk and then introduced himself as "Raoul." He never mentioned his last name, and I didn't press the matter.
>
> Raoul seemed to wrap himself in mystery. He spoke in loose terms, and he answered questions with generalities or not at all. His conversation drifted like a cool fog. I was not interested in making a lifelong friend. I was trying to make sure I didn't wind up back in the Missouri Prison,

and Raoul's personality wasn't of much interest to me. Besides, his pose was one familiar to me. I'd used it before myself, especially in prison. I'd known guys like Raoul for years. As we talked and drank, I sensed that I had a potential ally. Over the next few days, I often talked to Raoul at the Neptune Tavern, each of us trying to keep the other at arm's length but finally striking a bargain. He'd help me get travel documents if I'd assist him in moving contraband (drugs) across the border.

Around the first of August 1967, the two met again at the Neptune Tavern where they made a deal, whereby drugs concealed under the back seat and in the springs were taken across the border in Ray's car while driving alone on two different occasions and on two consecutive days. Raoul got out of Ray's car at the border city of Windsor, Canada, and traveled by bus where they met near the border crossing on the US side. On the second crossing, Smith, or "Raoul," left by bus into Detroit to dispose of the drugs. After the disposal, they met again for Ray's payoff. Raoul gave Ray $1,500, and they made another deal whereby Ray was to travel alone in his Plymouth to a designated motel room in Birmingham, Alabama. He was to wait there for further instructions to arrive by general delivery mail. He would receive a date to travel to Nuevo Laredo, Mexico. Ray would receive a large sum of money for once again carrying drugs across the border into the United States. Ray used the alias "Eric Galt," which was known to Raoul.

After being in Birmingham for a few days, Ray received a letter from Raoul to meet at a specific time and place near the Birmingham Post Office.

At the meeting, they discussed about Ray needing another car. The Plymouth was almost shot and needed repairs. Ray soon found a yellow 1966 Mustang, and Raoul paid him $2,000 to buy it with. Before Raoul left; he gave Ray another $500 to buy a movie camera and $1,000 in cash for expenses on the future trip to Mexico. Raoul said that he would notify Ray by general delivery mail of the time and place to meet in Nuevo Laredo. Raoul also gave Ray a New Orleans phone number in case Ray needed anything before going to Mexico. After waiting in Birmingham for almost a month without hearing from Raoul, Ray decided to call the New Orleans number. A strange voice answered telling James Earl Ray to call another number whereby he did talk to Raoul about the trip to Mexico.

Ray left Birmingham on the sixth of October 1967 by way of New Orleans. He called the number again while in New Orleans, and the same strange voice answered saying that Raoul had just left for Mexico by car. Ray then drove to Nuevo Laredo to a prearranged motel some two miles into the interior of Mexico. Raoul must have been on the lookout for Ray because he came to Ray's room thirty minutes after Ray's arrival. Raoul switched spare tires with Ray, and together they made a crossing into Laredo where Raoul directed Ray to drive to an isolated spot where the spare tire was removed and put into the trunk of a waiting car. This car was thought to be a Chevy and was driven by a dark-complexioned Hispanic man. This all took place at night. Back at the motel that night while Raoul and the stranger drove off together, Ray spent a peaceful night awaiting the return of the two men.

The two men arrived and directed Ray to follow them into the interior of Mexico past the twelve-mile checkpoint. There they made another spare tire "switcheroo" at an isolated spot. Raoul gave Ray another $2,000, saying he was still trying to get a passport to Europe or Africa by using a false ID for Ray. Raoul then gave Ray a new number to call in New Orleans if and when Ray would like to do more business with him. All the while, Raoul was promising to act on a new ID and passport for Ray.

At this point in time, around October 11, 1967, Ray decided to live it up in Mexico. He went to Acapulco and various other towns before deciding to go to California. He arrived in Los Angeles on November 19, 1967. While he hid in cheap hotels and bars, he met a woman who wanted to travel to New Orleans with two small children for a visit with relatives and friends.

By mid-December of 1967, Ray was getting short of money again, so he called Raoul's number in New Orleans. Sure enough, a stranger answered saying that he would have Raoul call him back. Ray then took the woman and kids to New Orleans, arriving around the fifteenth of December 1967. He met Raoul who gave Ray another $500 in cash for the return trip to LA. Ray, with the woman and kids, returned to

LA on the twentieth of December. He was to await another letter from Raoul when another deal could be arranged. Ray got some odd jobs between the twentieth of December 1967 and mid-March 1968. During this time, he checked the mail quite often to meet him on March 23, 1968, in Birmingham where Ray formerly rented an apartment in the cheap side of town. Raoul said he was now in the gunrunning business and wanted Ray to purchase a sample gun (rifle) to be shown to prospective buyers located in Memphis, Tennessee. In order to keep on the move, they decided to go to Atlanta. There they rented an apartment at 113 Fourteenth Street Nebraska. They talked about gunrunning out of Mexico. Raoul left for Miami, Florida, and returned on March 29, 1968. They left Atlanta, each in their own car, and went back to the rented apartment in Birmingham where Ray bought a rifle at a pawnshop. It was a Remington 30-06 with a scope. Raoul left for New Orleans again, saying that he would meet Ray in Memphis on April 2 at the De Soto Motel on Highway 51. The next day, they went together and rented a room for Ray at 422 1/2 Main Street. The shot that killed Martin Luther King Jr. was fired from this room.

The text above in bold type and quotation marks was the information obtained from James Earl Ray's book titled *Who killed Martin Luther King? The True Story by the Alleged Assassin*, published by National Press Books.

This book is well worth reading and a must for the conspiracy enthusiast.

# CHAPTER 4

# Raoul's Whereabouts

In the previous chapter, a time-lapse existed between December 18, 1967, and mid-March 1968 while Ray was waiting in Los Angeles. In my investigation, I learned why there was a three-month time-lapse and what Raoul's activities were during that period.

My wife and I had planned to spend the Easter holidays in Fort Worth visiting her nephew, three sisters, and brother. This was just after the assassination. On the Friday night before Easter in 1968, we drove to Fort Worth and spent the night at her nephew's home. On Saturday morning around ten o'clock, I telephoned the district attorney in Fort Worth to find out the name and telephone number of my stepson's attorney. We had just found out that James Smith had been released from the local county jail in late February. They had contacted his aunt, my wife's younger sister, in Fort Worth on about the third of March. He told her that he was on the run, fearing for his life. He gave no explanation but said that he might not have contact with any of his relatives for some time to come.

My wife had not heard from him since his call to her while in San Angelo in early July 1967. That was the last day he had the talk with our mutual friend, Rex Gavin.

When the media reported that two Mustangs had been observed at the scene of the crime and a report of a hoax transmission over police radio by a person representing himself as a local Memphis police officer, I had a gut feeling that it could well be my stepson.

He was so well versed in talking over the radio since he had been our local radio announcer in the past.

After learning of his release from the jail and meeting with my sister-in-law and with the gut feeling I had at the time, I contacted his attorney. I set up an appointment with him for 11:00 on Saturday morning. I learned a world of knowledge from him about James's activities from January through March 1968. I will relate the gist of our hour-long conversation I had with the attorney that morning. At that time in 1968, I was fifty-two years old. As I recalled, the attorney must have been fifteen years my senior, possibly more.

We introduced ourselves. He seemed to be in a very worried state of mind and was very cautious during our talk. He also made sure that I was, in fact, James Smith's stepfather. He reluctantly told me about James's activities during January and February of 1968.

He started out by saying that James Smith had been jailed locally on January 1968 for grand theft. Since it was his third offense, he had previously served two prison sentences, he would be considered a habitual criminal. With a life sentence staring him in the face and no ability to make bond, he had found himself in a desperate situation. He was desperate to find any possible way of obtaining his release. After spending about a month in jail, he contacted his boss in crime at Granbury. His boss came to see him in mid-February. During their conversation, he learned from his boss that he was going to fence some "hot" diamonds, worth $50,000, that he had stolen in Houston. The fence would take place in Dallas in the near future. I'm sure his boss did not realize the desperate situation James was in. James figured out immediately how he might get released.

James immediately called the local district attorney and, after the attorney agreed the release in exchange for help in recovering the diamonds, relayed his findings. The deal was consummated, and James was released without bond. With the permission of James, two detectives kept constant surveillance on his personal habitat and activities. On some pretext for his release, he contacted his boss in Granbury, stating that he would be happy to accompany him to Dallas for the fencing of the stolen diamonds. The boss agreed wholehearted, not knowing it was a "set up" or double cross. About the twenty-sixth or twenty-seventh of February, James and his boss proceeded to drive from Fort Worth to Dallas with the two detectives following. This is a twenty-mile trip on I-30 with lots of traffic. The detectives had to trail very closely in the same lane in order not to get lost. Arriving on the outskirts of Dallas, Mr. Flannigan, the boss, became suspicious of the car tailgating him for twenty miles. He pulled over to the curb and stopped to let the tailgater go on his way. Instead, the detectives stopped their car and jumped out with guns drawn. While searching Flannigan's car, the detectives found the diamonds and arrested them both on the spot.

Both of them were sent to Houston where they were charged with grand theft. Mr. Flannigan's bond was set at $50,000. The district attorney in Fort Worth had made previous arrangements with the Houston authorities for bond to be set at $1,000 for James. The bond for James was put up by his attorney, and he was released on the second of March. Mr. Flannigan had been out on bond for about two weeks at the time of my talk with the attorney representing James. The lawyer was very worried at this point and time because he had not heard from or seen James since his release. It looked like the lawyer was stuck with the bond. He was also very worried about the life of James Allen Smith since he knew at the time that James was number one on Flannigan's hit list.

The lawyer had represented both James and Flannigan. Flannigan had obviously relayed his intentions after his release from the Houston jail. As you will find out in the chapter to follow, the autopsy report from Austin figured that James died in mid to late April 1968, and his death might well have occurred during the Easter holidays at the approximate time of my meeting with his attorney.

I know one thing, this attorney was a very worried and frustrated man. I sensed that he knew more that he would tell. I did not tell my wife of the meeting. The following four pages are copies held by the FBI and released under the Freedom of Information Act in regard to the interview by an FBI agent with Smith's attorney on the twenty-fifth of April 1968. According to the autopsy report, at this point, James Smith had already been murdered.

# CHAPTER 5

# The FBI File on James Allen Smith

I previously mentioned the releases of the FBI papers to me regarding Smith's attorney and his FBI interview. I will first submit the one and only report that the FBI received from the Tarrant County Sheriff's Office. In this report, Smith voluntarily appeared with his attorney for questioning.

He flatly denied any involvement in stolen cars and was released. This happened on the twenty-fourth of February 1967, thirteen months before the King assassination.

In other papers released by the FBI, he was a suspect in stolen cars as early as 1966. He was never apprehended by the FBI.

You will note that they were still looking for him in May and June of 1968, with the Dallas FBI headquarters not knowing that his remains were lying in a remote pasture near Granbury, Texas, some thirty miles southwest of Fort Worth.

According to the papers that were released, you will note that there was no mention of Smith from the twenty-fourth of February 1967 until May 1968, after his murder. The question remains; what is so important about not releasing the other four hundred odd pages on a supposedly small-time hoodlum?

In my opinion, it can only mean direct contact with a branch of the FBI in New Orleans. There could also be some information regarding the Cadillac's episode with the SCLC since he had a record of dealing in stolen cars. Bud Fensterwald gathered some information, whereby Hosea Williams, head of the SCLC, was accused of having received some stolen Cadillacs in 1966 and 1967. For various reasons, he was not indicted. According to Rex Gavin's talk with me, however, Smith did deliver these Caddys to the SCLC and did not receive the money from them.

The following was the information contained in the document, dated February 24, 1967, from the Tarrant County Sheriff's Office:

> James Allen Smith appeared voluntarily at the Tarrant County Sheriff's Office, accompanied by his attorney. Smith and his attorney were shown the official credentials of the special agent and Smith was advised by the special agent that he desired to question him regarding several alleged violations of Federal statutes involving the inter-state transportation of stolen automobiles. Smith was advised of his rights and read and executed a statement of his rights.

Smith stated that all he would say about any allegations regarding stolen cars was that if anyone said he was involved with stolen cars, they were "trying to put the beef on me that I had no part of." He refused to make any further statement.

This chapter contains partial files released by the FBI to Glen R. Tennis in August 1992 under the Freedom of Information Act.

The FBI has 542 pages of material on James Allen Smith dated back to 1966. The release on 124 pages deals only with Smith as being a suspect in stolen cars, etc. in which he was not prosecuted for various reasons.

The following pages deal in interviews with Smith's attorney by the FBI and police officials alike during the time of Smith's demise, which the autopsy revealed to have happened in mid-April of 1968.

The remaining 418 pages that the FBI refused to release could be information, dates, etc., relating to events that occurred when Smith surfaced to accept the $50,000 offer from the FBI. My belief could be that Smith dealt with the FBI undercover agents in New Orleans who was taking direct orders from Hoover.

You will note that James Earl Ray called New Orleans several times in order to contact Raoul. Then Raoul went back to New Orleans after the purchase of the rifle, meeting Ray the following day in Memphis. His going to New Orleans, in my opinion, was to pick up the two men who Ray described as strangers, and who I believe were the "hit man" and FBI agent. I believe these were the men seen by Ray in the downstairs bar in the flophouse a short time before the assassination.

**Bold text** inside of brackets ([]) were blocked out in the FBI report and were reconstructed by the author.

[**Smith's attorney**] has known James Allen Smith for about two years. Smith has been in a lot of trouble and has a long arrest record. In the Summer of 1967 Smith was in the Tarrant County Jail on four charges of burglary, forgery, and theft. He contacted [**his attorney**] on several occasions to represent him and get him out on bond. Smith could not raise any money and finally raised a total of $400. [**Smith's attorney**] had set a fee of $700. Smith told [**his attorney**] he owned some property in Houston and had some assets in Houston and if he could get out he could easily raise the other $300 and pay him in full. [**Smith's attorney**] finally agreed to make the bond, and Smith was released. He talked to Smith after he was released from jail. Smith was going to Houston and liquidate some assets and pay [**his attorney**] the balance of his fee for making his bonds. [**His attorney**] never saw or heard from Smith until 2/29/68, when he read in the paper that Smith was arrested with [**his crime boss, Mr. Flannigan. Flannigan and**] Smith were immediately taken to Houston, Texas, to face a number of [**felony**] charges.

[**Smith's attorney**] went to the District Attorney's Office in Fort Worth to get off the bonds of Smith [**and Flannigan. Smith's attorney**] did not plan to make any bond for Smith in Houston, Texas. The District Attorney in Fort Worth and Houston, along with state officers asked his assistance in the matter, and he made bond for Smith in Houston on about 3/4/68. He has not seen nor heard from Smith since then. He has tried to locate Smith through all known contacts in Fort Worth but has not been successful. He had heard rumors that Smith might have been killed [**by the Flannigan gang or their "hit man"**]. He has also heard [**Smith's attorney**] related that Smith is a chronic liar, boastful, and exaggerates stories about himself. He stated Smith is a lowlife police character and will do most anything to raise a few dollars.

[**Smith's attorney**] had never heard of Smith having any dealings with Martin Luther King and never heard Smith mention "South Christian Conference." He has talked about everything else but this matter to [**him**]. Smith claimed he could do nearly anything on earth. [**He**] did not trust or believe Smith very much prior to last time he made bonds for him. He stated at this time he would not believe Smith "on a stack of Bibles." Smith has been involved in car theft, but [**his attorney**] never heard of him being involved in Georgia or deep South. [**He**] is still trying to locate Smith as they have indicated they would call his case in Houston, Texas, in the near future.

[**He**] related if he should receive any information as to the whereabouts of Smith, he would notify the Fort Worth RA.

[**Personal name**] Texas Ranger, advised on 5/2/68, he had not heard from Smith and had not been able to develop any information as to his whereabouts. He stated Smith might have been knocked off [**by the Flannigan gang. He**] knows Smith well and has talked to a number of contacts of Smith but has not been able to locate Smith. He stated Smith talks big, brags, tells big stories, and is one of the biggest liars in the world. [**Personal name**] Detective, Fort Worth Police Department, was contacted on 5/6/68. He advised he is well acquainted with James Allen Smith. He has made inquires through all his sources but has not turned up any information on Smith. He related Smith could be buried [**blocked out text unknown**] or Smith might be taking advantage of the situation, has left Fort Worth, and is laying low. [**The detective**] had never heard of Smith being involved in anything in Georgia or Alabama. He further related he would not believe Smith or any of the big stories he tells.

[**The detective**] was recontacted on 5/7/68, at which time he advised he had not received any information as to the whereabouts of Smith. The case at Houston has been called, but he obtained a postponement for 60 days. No further investigation being conducted to locate Smith Armed and Dangerous.

---

# C H A P T E R   6

---

# The Assassination of Martin Luther King Jr.

At the end of chapter 3, we find Raoul and Ray together on the day of the assassination at the flophouse where a room had been rented for Ray, alias "Eric Galt." After Ray had checked out at the Desoto Motel, he rented a room at the Rebel Inn where he picked up the 30-06 rifle, saying he should move again to the flophouse at 422 1/2 Main Street. This all happened on the day of the assassination. Raoul's pretext to Ray was the secret meeting of two expected gun buyers without Ray being present as ordered and told to Ray by Raoul.

When Ray left the Rebel Inn, he was instructed to go to 422 1/2 Main Street where Raoul would meet him at Jim's Bar on the ground floor. Ray walked a short distance along Main Street and accidentally walked into the wrong bar. He thought he was in Jim's Bar until he noticed two strangers intently eyeing him. He asked the attendant in charge if he was actually in Jim's Bar. The attendant replied that he was not; Jim's was up the street away. He then went back to his yellow Mustang and parked behind another yellow mustang in front of Jim's Bar. When he walked into the bar to meet Raoul, the two strangers whom he just encountered in the bar down the street were sitting at the same table talking with Raoul. They were engaged in conversation with Raoul. Raoul immediately got up and went with Ray to his room where he saw the rifle still in the box that it came in when he had purchased it at the pawnshop.

Raoul then informed Ray that he should leave for a while, take in a movie, or get lost until after the gun sale, in which he expected the buyer to show up at anytime. Ray left at 4:00 PM, expected to eat a bite before going to a nearby movie.

While eating, he suddenly realized that a previous flat tire in the spare rack had not been fixed. So instead of going to a movie, he went back to his yellow Mustang, which at the time was parked behind an identical yellow Mustang. Unknown to Raoul, he drove his Mustang to a nearby service station where the tire was repaired. He then filled the car with gasoline and started back to the flophouse to park it again, in hopes of walking to a nearby movie to pass some more time.

However, on the trip back, he was forced by the local police to detour. They were not letting any motorists to go down South Main Street. Ray then turned on his radio, and a police bulletin was saying that a man in a yellow Mustang was a suspect in the shooting, which happened just moments before.

According to James Earl Ray's book, he knew nothing about King's presence in Memphis or where he was staying. In fact, he could care less about King and his activities. After all, he was an escaped convict trying to survive without being caught and sent back to prison. As you will recall, King and company were ordered by police authorities to move from another motel to the motel adjacent to the flophouse during the night of the second and third of April. At that point in time, Ray was spending the night at the Rebel Inn some distance from 422 1/2 Main Street and did not know of King's presence in Memphis.

Ray's only interest at the time was assisting Raoul in gunrunning in the hopes of making big money so as to escape from the United States to some foreign country using false identity papers. In his book, Ray mentioned this time and time again. It was constantly on his mind.

During the exact time frame that James Earl Ray was getting his flat fixed, Martin Luther King was killed. Why wasn't the person who fixed the flat for James Earl Ray found and made to testify? It was also during this same time frame that the famous hoax police radio report given by someone impersonating the Memphis Police was given. Whoever it was that was impersonating an officer on the radio said that he was in high-speed pursuit of a yellow Mustang and thought it to be driven by King's assassin.

After reading the preceding chapters, you can well see how Raoul was able to gain the confidence of Ray and how he set Ray up to become the "fall guy" without Ray suspecting what was actually going on. When the rifle was found in the original box with Ray's fingerprints on it carefully left on Main Street in Memphis in the box, along with Ray's prison radio. The radio had Ray's identification number etched into it. You can easily see that Raoul made sure of this by having him handle the gun on inspection after the purchase in Birmingham. After Ray's first and only trial, when he was found guilty in the most hurried trial in history, he soon recanted his guilty plea and declared he was "set up" by Raoul. He has never been able to get another trial even though he tried time and again since 1970 to obtain one.

In the following chapters, I will give the details pertaining to the dates, times, etc. to show the reader how James Allen Smith, in my opinion, was the person that James Earl Ray knew only as "Raoul." I will also show the motive and desperation on Raoul's part.

I will portray step by step, date by date, how Raoul went about setting up Mr. Ray to become the victim in the assassination, allowing the assassination committee to come to the conclusion in their final report that a person named "Raoul" never existed and that Ray only concealed the box the rifle came in from the story for whatever reason. But if the reader will only read the book by James Earl Ray entitled *Who Killed Martin Luther King? The True Story by the Alleged Assassin*, I'm sure you can see why I wrote this book.

# CHAPTER 7

# The Death of James Allen Smith

James Allen Smith was born on July 4, 1935, and died on April 7, 1968.

On the morning of July 6, 1968, while working in my shop at my business, I received a long distance telephone call. The man said he was the autopsy man in Austin, Texas. He asked if I had a stepson named James Allen Smith. I said yes but had not seen him for some time. He said that he had a corpse in his possession, which was found by two lady hikers on July Fourth. The only ID was an empty billfold with a card of identification and a name of only James Allen Smith. He said he had checked the Huntsville state prison and found that their records showed a James Allen Smith had served two prison terms in the institution in the early 1960s. Their records also showed my address and telephone number. He said that his purpose in calling me was to get a positive identification.

"You see," he said, "this corpse had been lying on a remote ranch site under a clump of trees, exposed to the elements."

He estimated that the person died from a single bullet to the forehead and that it had occurred sometime in April. The body was found some six or so miles southeast of Granbury, Texas, in a remote part of a ranch. The clothes were still on the corpse.

I said to him that one leg was shorter than the other due to an early childhood disease of polio and that he had some dental work done while in prison. He said that he had already checked the dental records at Huntsville, and they had proved positive. He also said that one leg on the body was shorter than the other.

"How about two socks on the short foot?" I asked.

"Yes, that checks out too," he said.

He then told me that in his opinion, the corpse was indeed that of my stepson. He said that the corpse would be sent back to the Granbury funeral parlor, and we could go from there. Graveside services were held on Saturday, July 13, at the Myra Cemetery, about ten miles west of Gainesville. The arrangements were handled by Carrol Funeral and Mertin Funeral Home in Granbury. He was buried next to his father, and it was closed casket funeral. None of his relatives or friends looked inside. Farther on in this book, one will see that now I had wished a thousand times that I had looked to see if there was indeed a corpse in the casket. Personally, I believed it to be James A. Smith in this particular grave.

At least a big burden had been lifted from our shoulders by his untimely death. Now, we could go on living a more natural and contented life without being continually embarrassed, financially and otherwise. His death was, of course, a shock to everyone because he had been murdered by person or people unknown at the time. Furthermore, it was still an unsolved murder at the time of this writing in 1992. In fact, it may never be solved as in the case of Martin Luther King Jr. and John F. Kennedy.

Over the past twenty-four years, so many witnesses and people with vital knowledge have died. For instance, my wife died on November 2, 1986, and Rex Gavin and J. Edgar Hoover both in 1972. Also the whereabouts, dead or alive, of my stepson's ex-lawyer was unknown. Also, the whereabouts of James's ex-wife, Kitty Anderson, was unknown.

Things did not come together in this puzzle of the century until I had read James Earl Ray's book, *Who Killed Martin Luther King? The True Story by the Alleged Assassin.*

However, now I can present the limited knowledge that I have been able to obtain over the past twenty-four years of investigation. I think I owe it to my wife and the world if I can help to bring out the truth.

After the funeral on July 1968 and after the local FBI had given me their final report on August 1968, I had to let matters rest in limbo and let history and nature take its course. But in the summer of 1977, while the assassination committee was holding its hearing in regard to Kennedy and King, an event happened in the lives of my wife and myself that has never been revealed to anyone. This was partially for fear for our own lives and because we were so confused by not knowing the truth or whom to believe.

═══════════════════════

# C H A P T E R   8

═══════════════════════

# The Sudden Visit of Kitty Anderson

In the early summer of 1975, while my wife and I were eating breakfast, she developed a severe pain under her left arm in the heart area. I rushed her to a local hospital where she was diagnosed as having a heart attack. She remained in the hospital for about a month. The doctor suggested that someone should be with her at home for a year or so until her complete recovery. As no one was available at the time, it meant that yours truly would have to be that person.

Other than the actual semiweekly auctions, my wife and I practically ran my place of business by ourselves. A young ambitious employee of mine offered to buy me out after learning of my wife's condition. On August 1975, I sold out, lock, stock, and barrel. I was sixty years old at the time and thought that it was time to semiretire and take it more slowly in the future.

For the next year, I stayed and worked out of my house, wholesaling used furniture to old buyers of mine and to the new owner of my former business. I would buy from various wholesale dealers in the metroplex of Dallas and Fort Worth. I had a large trailer and pickup truck in which I would make a one-day trip to Fort Worth and back. My wife recovered by Christmas and would go with me. She would stay overnight with my sister or her relatives. My wholesale business grew so much; I was forced to rent a large room at a storage rent-all. I soon outgrew this building and rented a large warehouse at the edge of town. I ran this business from 1982 to 1988 when I semiretired again.

Around the first of August in 1977, my wife and I received an unexpected local telephone call. The person calling was Kitty Anderson, our former daughter-in-law, the ex-wife of James Allen Smith. We had not seen or heard from her since the divorce in 1958. She said that she was in San Angelo on business, selling advanced tickets to sponsored local business firms for a three-night stand at our local coliseum by a famous Nashville music organization.

She and her association were staying at a local motel furnished by the music group. She came by and invited us to have lunch. In our conversation, she wanted my wife and I to help her in selling tickets by telephone since we were so well acquainted with everyone here. She also wanted me to do the collections on a commission basis. It was a slack time for me, so we accepted, both of us making good extra money.

Her next stop was in Abilene, so we both did the same job there. After this was over, my business at home needed me, so I took off. This was in September of 1977. My wife, however, liked her job so well; she continued working at various cities in Texas and two more in Tennessee until she decided to come back home on November 1977. We conversed two or three times a week by telephone during the time she was gone.

Our ex-daughter-in-law spent the night with us when she brought my wife home. While going to bed that night, my wife told me she had something important to tell me that happened to be bothering her to no end. The following is the gist of our conversation.

"As you might well know by now," she said, "Kitty likes her drinks at night for relaxation after a hard day's work. Well, one night at Dalhart, Texas, while we were relaxing and chatting and she had several drinks under her belt, she suddenly asked me if I knew why she had come back into my life. I said, 'No, why?' 'Well you see, I still love James, and I must tell you something. He is not dead but is living in Argentina, South America. I can't give you any details other than he is living under a false identity. The FBI did this for him for a reason that I cannot reveal to you. Someday in the future, when things for him cool down and are forgotten, don't be surprised when he returns and walks in on you.' But I told her we had a funeral for him on July 13, 1968, and this just couldn't be true. She said she would bet her last nickel that either the corpse was not that of James or maybe no one at all."

At that point in time, my wife was so confused that she did not know what to believe but hoped that Kitty was right. To me at the time, it looked like a brand-new ball game. As Kitty was fixing to leave and go out the door, I confronted her with the following question: "You say James is in Argentina. Did he have anything to do with the assassination of Martin Luther King Jr.?"

The startled expression on her face was something to behold. She stared back at me as only a concerned ex-convict could do. She abruptly opened the door and slammed it shut behind her without saying yes or no. Neither my wife nor I have seen or heard of her to this day.

To me, this was a dead giveaway since I had known her quite well. I think I hit the nail on the head, especially since she has never made contact with us from that time on. She had promised to write often, but to this day, we have not heard a word from her. I do know that she is not working in Nashville and no one there seems to know of her whereabouts. With her being an ex-convict, I believe she might be using an alias since leaving San Angelo in 1977.

The house select committee on assassinations regarding Kennedy and King were holding hearings at this point in time. The gist of the final report on King stated that they believe Ray shot King. It was likely, however, that a conspiracy could have existed, but they were unable to pursue the matter for lack of evidence.

A St. Louis man, Russell George Byers, swore to the committee under oath that he rejected a $50,000 offer from the lawyer, John Sutherland, to kill King. Representative Louis Stokes, a committee man, noticed that the FBI learned in 1974 of the possible St. Louis conspiracy and the $50,000 reward but lost the information in a filing error. In my judgment, this is another cover-up by the FBI. When the leak of the reward was released to the underworld, Ray was in prison and could not have done anything about it if he had wanted to. His time and efforts were devoted to escaping jail and hiding and a desire to get papers to go to Africa or any overseas country. Hence, the meeting and activities with Raoul after their first meeting in Montreal, Canada. Ray was desperate to find an ally to help him out, so consequently, he teamed up with Raoul who promised this help. He also made a lot of money working with Raoul who was in the process of gaining Ray's confidence for the double cross in setting Ray up as the "fall guy." I must admit that my stepson would have been a master at this endeavor. He was a confident man deluxe. I knew him quite well.

Ray's onetime lawyer, Mark Lane, was convinced that a conspiracy existed and that the FBI was the central figure behind it. But Lane's hands were tied because neither he nor Ray could ever produce the evidence that Raoul existed. One can see the problem with producing evidence of Raoul's existence. Raoul was in hiding until he was murdered shortly after King's demise, and during all the meetings between Ray and Raoul over the preceding eight months, Ray only learned Raoul's first name. Raoul had always concealed his true identity and address. Therefore, the assassination committee, and everyone else, came up empty-handed, making it look like Ray was lying. However, after reading Ray's book, I am convinced that there was indeed a "Raoul" and that his description, manners, actions, and location at certain dates and times correspond with my stepson, James Allen Smith.

The following reasons are why I believe that Raoul was, in reality, James Allen Smith.

James Allen Smith's qualifications for prime suspect are the following:

1. Motive—vow to assassinate King because of the loss of the stolen Cadillacs to the SCLC.
2. Reasons of identity:
    a) Fits James Earl Ray's description of Raoul
    b) James Allen Smith loved the name Raoul, which was the name used by the man who set up Ray.

3. Past criminal record:
   a) Two-time prison inmate at Huntsville, Texas, from 1962 to 1965 for car theft and forgery
   b) Member of the Flannigan Gang from 1965 to 1968
   c) Rented a building in Fort Worth for processing stolen cars, mainly new Cadillacs and Mustangs from 1966 to 1967
   d) Associated only with underworld friends and allies
   e) Double-crossed his gang's boss
4. James Smith's personal car was a yellow 1966 or 1967 Mustang with a two-way police radio, just like the Memphis police were trying to stoke; a committee man noticed that the FBI found the car immediately after the assassination. Witnesses stated that two yellow Mustangs were located at the scene of the shooting. James Earl Ray stated that he owned one of the cars and Raoul owned the other.
5. Education and employment background:
   a) An A student in elementary and high school and college
   b) Number one disk jockey and announcer on KGKL, San Angelo in 1957
   c) An A-1 salesman and con man
6. Attitude toward life and the world:
   a) Smith believed that the world was a sucker for taking by any means or methods.
   b) No regard for anyone he might hurt financially, morally or otherwise.
   c) Selfish in regard to his own finances.
   d) Felt self-pity in refusing to share and share alike with brothers and sisters.
   e) Blamed parents and grandparents for his upbringing as a child.
   f) Determined to show the world that he could overcome any money problems by underworld activities.
7. Was murdered by person or persons unknown in late April 1968, just two weeks after the King assassination. Both

Bud Fensterwald and James Smith's stepfather believe that he was murdered, either directly or indirectly, by the FBI.

8.  Told his ex-wife that the FBI was sending him to Argentina with a new identity.

9.  The hoax radio report of a Memphis police officer chasing a yellow Mustang is exactly the type of thing James Smith would do.

10. Facts revealed to James Smith's stepfather by mutual friends.

11. James Allen Smith's whereabouts and activities correspond with those of Raoul as described in James Earl Ray's book.

12. Document containing four hundred pages of information on James Allen Smith in the FBI archives; this document was requested by Bud Fensterwald and James Lesar, former attorneys for James Earl Ray.

To date, the FBI has refused to release the complete document to the attorneys. Part of the document was released to Smith's stepfather. However, the pages covering the time period around the King assassination were not released.

# Conclusion Reached by the Author

In the years since the King assassination, I have gathered information and data and put everything in consecutive order. I will try, to the best of my abilities, to present the events related to the assassination. In order to do so, one must assume that the following facts, which I have presented in previous chapters, are true and correct:

1. Raoul was James Allen Smith, my stepson.
2. Ray really was "set up" by Raoul.
3. The FBI and Raoul were conspirators.
4. J. Edgar Hoover and company hated King and wanted him out of the way.
5. James Smith vowed to kill King for monetary reasons.

Keeping these facts in mind, the following is what I believe happened. Some say that sometime in early 1967, the FBI put out word to the underworld that a $50,000 reward would be paid to anyone to kill King. It was about this same time that James Smith lost his fortune through the "Cadillac's sale" to an organization headed by King and his associates.

When Raoul, or my stepson, had the meeting in early July 1967, with our mutual friend, Rex Gavin, he told him that a plan was already in the making to have King assassinated. I believe Hoover and my stepson were in the early stages of the process. I believe that Hoover and Raoul were putting the final touches to the assassination plan when my stepson was released from the Houston jail on February 29, 1968. Raoul already had Ray under his thumb for a double cross. It was also about this time that Raoul found himself in a corner due to his double cross of his boss on the diamond episode, hence, the "hit" was out on him. Things were coming to a head fast and furious for Raoul after his release from the Houston jail. In my horse sense way of thinking, I believe that Raoul told Hoover of his desperate situation and that Hoover promised to send him to Argentina with a new identity after the assassination was completed.

According to Ray's book, on that afternoon, just before the assassination, he had encountered the same two strange men in two different bars. He last saw them talking to Raoul in Jim's Bar, which is on the ground floor of the building from which the shot was fired.

Since neither my stepson nor Ray were ever sharpshooters, I would naturally presume that at least one of the strangers was a paid "hit man." I personally believe that one of these men shot King. They could have used gloves in order to protect Ray's fingerprints on the rifle. They could have also used their own weapon, another new 30-06. There was some controversy over whether the rifle, which the FBI found in Ray's room, was in fact the murder weapon. With Hoover in control of the investigation, almost anything could have happened.

At any rate, the gun bought by Ray was left at the scene of the murder, dismantled and in a box, with Ray's fingerprints on it. If Ray did the shooting, why would he be so dumb to leave the murder weapon behind to positively identify him? This makes no sense to me whatsoever. Hence, my belief that Ray was double-crossed and set up as the "fall guy."

I believe that Raoul and the two strangers left immediately after the shooting with Raoul using his police radio to transmit the hoax of an officer chasing a yellow or white Mustang. This hoax report would be exactly the type of thing that my stepson would think of. I knew him well, and remember, being a former disk jockey, he had experience talking on the radio. Hearing of this hoax was, in fact, the first hint to me that my stepson was involved. That, in conjunction with the fact that Ray said that he was set up by a person known only as "Raoul," intensified my gut feeling. Then when Rex Gavin stated the motive given to him by my stepson, I was more positive than ever that I was on the right track.

It was not until the conversation with my wife and former daughter-in-law on November 1977 that I could see the connection between Hoover and my stepson. I had a gut feeling all along from the day of the assassination that a connection between the two had existed, but there was no proof.

I think that my ex-daughter-in-law was mistaken in believing that James Smith was sent to Argentina immediately after the assassination. According to her, she talked to James Smith by telephone in mid-April 1968 about the FBI transferring him to Argentina. I think, however, that Hoover knew of the "hit" out on Smith by his former boss in crime. So why not have the gang do the dirty work? This could easily be accomplished by informing the gang of Smith's whereabouts while he was waiting for his new identity paperwork to be processed.

With Ray under surveillance and sure to be caught at the appropriate time and Raoul murdered by whomever, Hoover would be home free. He would never be suspected as even an accomplice, let alone as the main conspirator.

First, my stepson double-crossed his boss, then he double-crossed Ray. Then he was double-crossed by the "big boss," Hoover. What goes around comes around. Both Hoover and my stepson are dead, taking their secrets with them. James Earl Ray is currently serving a life sentence for the one crime he didn't commit, without knowing the identity of Raoul. However, with his past record of crime, he must now feel at home in prison, only hoping that new evidence will produce a new trial when the FBI records were revealed at some later date.

So it came down to one simple, yet profound, question: Who killed Dr. Martin Luther King Jr.? Was it Raoul? Was it one of the strangers with Raoul that day? Or, as we have been led to believe by our own government, was it simply James Earl Ray? What do you think?

# CHAPTER 10

## Hoover the Great Conspirator

When I write about anyone, I feel I must put myself in their shoes, so to speak, in order to realize their way of life, actions, and thoughts.

So it is when I try to portray the lifestyle of J. Edgar Hoover. I was nine years old in 1924 when Hoover took over the office as head of the FBI. He had complete control of this office until his demise. He was restricted for only a short period during his reign. This was when Attorney General Robert Kennedy, who was appointed by his brother, John F. Kennedy, president of the USA from 1960 through 1963.

Hoover was a bachelor, and his sole interest in life was tied completely by his job, day and night, week by week, month by month, year by year, until his death in 1972. For thirty-six years, from 1924 through 1960, he ran his office to suit himself without any outside interference. He had become a king, a legend, and a tyrant in his capacity as head of the FBI. Wiretaps, surveillances, undercover operations, the legality of which was of no concern to him. Subordinates had to realize that the order of the day was to do the job by any means possible, legal or not, if they wanted to keep their jobs. It was a way of life for Hoover who could see no wrong in any actions or methods he might choose to employ. With this attitude and way of life, Hoover became annoyed with Martin Luther King Jr. and his protest marches, speeches, etc. I truly believe that J. Edgar Hoover despised all black people. He considered them an inferior race of people who should have been content to assume an inferior place in our society. He branded King a communist and hounded him to no end, using illegal tactics, wiretaps, and false imprisonments.

By 1960, Hoover was getting out of hand, and the president did something about it. He appointed his little brother to the office of attorney general. He had power to exercise control over J. Edgar Hoover and the way that policy was administered by the powerful agency of the United States government. Robert Kennedy had several meetings with Hoover and put a damper on many of Hoover's activities that he deemed illegal.

Put yourself in Hoover's shoes for a moment. After being a king of the FBI for thirty-six years, how would you react to this situation? I can hear Hoover talking about the appointed attorney general. He's still "wet behind the ears." *How can someone with as little experience as Robert Kennedy have the gall to try and tell an old pro like me how to do my job? How dare…* Can't you see the hatred developing over the next few years?

Hoover was, however, a very smart man with lots of expertise and experience. He knew that he could solve his problem with the Kennedys without having himself come under suspicion by paying the underworld to get the job done. I believe this was the case with Oswald and Sirhan Sirhan, as well as Raoul and Ray.

The general public was unaware of Hoover's activities in his later years and that he had become lord, king, and eventually a tyrant over the FBI. I have read several books by authors who knew Hoover well and who in turn wrote about his life and his service in the FBI. These descriptions of Hoover's life led me to believe that he was one-hundred-percent behind the three assassinations which occurred from 1963 to 1968. The opening of the archives may prove this to be true. Then again, we may never know or be able to prove the truth. Hoover was a master in covering his tracks by destroying incriminating evidence and the like. One thing we do know, however, is that John and Robert Kennedy and Martin Luther King Jr. were all enemies of Hoover.

# CHAPTER 11

# Why I Believe Hoover and Raoul Were Conspirators

Hoover and Raoul both had strong motives for wanting King assassinated. Ray, on the other hand, had no motives at all for wanting King dead.

When the underworld was informed of the $50,000 reward on King's life, I believe Raoul seized upon what he thought was a golden opportunity. He imagined himself killing two birds with one stone. He had actually seized a double-edged sword. He thought he could collect the huge reward and avenge himself for the loss suffered on the Cadillac deal at the same time. Best of all, he thought James Earl Ray would take the blame for it all. James did not know that the hunter would eventually become the hunted and the user would be used.

On the twenty-ninth of February 1968, we find two small-time hoodlums in similar situations. Ray was, and had been, on the run as a habitual criminal, especially after his jailbreak at the Missouri prison in 1967. James Allen Smith, or Raoul, was on the run, knowing that his life was at stake. He was on his former boss's "hit list." When all of these factors came together on March 1968, the master plan for the assassination became riper and riper until the final chapter in the life of Martin Luther King Jr.

These, my friends, are my sincere beliefs and convictions of how, why, and who were responsible in the assassination. Only intense investigations in the future by responsible and honest personnel can prove, or help prove, my beliefs.

I truly believe that James Allen Smith, deceased, was the person known to Ray only as Raoul. I believed that he did exist and did, in fact, set Ray up. By concealing his identity from Ray, Ray became the used. Raoul made it appear that Ray was lying. Raoul worked hand in hand with Hoover and company to execute the master plan to near perfection. There was one slight problem with the plan on the day of the execution. You will recall that Raoul thought that Ray had gone to a movie or bar to eat at about 4:00 PM on the day of the assassination. He thought that Ray had gone on foot and that Ray's car was still parked out front.

After the shooting, when Raoul and the two strangers tried to make their exit from the scene, they saw that Ray's Mustang was missing. I think they had planned on placing the rifle in Ray's car before leaving, so the "hot" weapon had to be left in the room or nearby where it was found soon afterward. It doesn't make any sense to me that Ray would have left the weapon in his room or next door where it would be found for sure. Who in their right mind would deliberately try to incriminate themselves in such a manner? If it had been found in his car, it would have been more convincing that Ray was the killer. Something more was needed to put suspicion on Ray. I believe that is the reason for the hoax radio report.

No one has ever reported seeing or identifying the getaway car used by Raoul and the two strangers. You can bet your life that the FBI took care of that situation. I also believe Raoul departed with his FBI partners to New Orleans to wait for his new identity papers and passport. While hiding there, he called his ex-wife, Kitty Anderson, and told her he was waiting to go to Argentina. I believe that by Hoover's order, Smith was betrayed or turned over to his former crime boss for execution.

No one has, and probably never will, lift a finger to solve the murder of my stepson. You can bet that the FBI is not at all interested as it would eventually involve them in the King assassination.

Some of you readers may think that I am a crackpot. Well, the following information might convince you otherwise.

There is an organization located at suite 510-918 F Street North West, Washington, DC, 20004, by the name "Assassination Archives and Research Center." This organization was founded by the attorney of James Earl Ray, Bud Fensterwald, who died suddenly of a heart attack in the spring of 1991. We had been in constant contact since August of 1990 by mail and in person. I have kept all of his correspondence to me, and he has returned all of my correspondence to him after making copies.

Bud made a special plane trip to my home in November 1990 where we discussed my investigations regarding my stepson. He came to the conclusion that we were on the right track. His sudden death four months later, however, has put our detective work in limbo. He did, however, find out about the stolen Caddys which had been in the possession of Hosea Williams who represented the SCLC headquarters in Atlanta from 1967 through 1968.

After reading Ray's book, one can readily see that Ray tried his best not to mention any names or addresses which might incriminate himself or any of his associates. The best example of this is when Bud Fensterwald had an interview with him on January 1991 at the prison he was serving at. When Bud showed him a nine-by-twelve photograph of James Allen Smith taken in 1957, some eleven years prior to the assassination, he refused to say yes, no, or maybe.

Bud and I thought that Ray might think that Raoul might still be alive. You can see why Ray has refused to identify any and all photos shown to him. The law of the underworld works whether you might be in or out of prison, especially if you were caught being a "snitch."

For some reason, not known or revealed by Ray, he was stabbed several times by inmates while in Petros prison in Tennessee. I suppose this incident has made a true believer out of him about underworld laws. Hence, he refused to identify any photos even though it could possibly warrant a new trial at some future date, which was the object of Bud's visit with him. Ray refused flatly to identify any photos because I feel, and Bud felt, that his life might be endangered if he tells too much. Even without this refusal on Ray's part, I am still convinced that James Allen Smith and Raoul are the same person and that he was murdered soon after the King assassination.

In my personal opinion, this episode regarding the identity of the conspirators is one of the largest FBI cover-ups of this decade.

# CHAPTER 12

# Conclusion

In conclusion, I will summarize the convictions that I now have that my stepson, James Allen Smith, alias Raoul, and J. Edgar Hoover and associates were conspirators in the King assassination.

By assuming that Hoover was the main conspirator and behind the whole episode from the very start, it is logical that we start on him first.

J. Edgar Hoover was appointed head of the FBI in 1924 during the Calvin Coolidge administration and during the time when the outlaws, desperados, and underworld figures were running amuck in our society. From 1924 through 1972, he and his staff did a superb job in eliminating such characters as Al Capone, John Dillinger, and other members of the mafia. He served under eight consecutive presidents. This is a legend in itself. No wonder the general public considered him a hero never to be distrusted.

But history has proven over and over that a person such as Hoover, in authority for a long period of time, often becomes a tyrant or dictator. During Hoover's reign, he was unchecked until the Kennedy administration in 1960. During that time, his word became law with no questions asked. It was of no concern to him the effects of illegal activities to anyone at any time or place. By this point in time, he had become a master in gaining his objectives, legal or otherwise. Hence, the rebuff by Robert Kennedy, the newly appointed US attorney general. Hoover's attitude was natural hidden anger that grew day by day until the Kennedy brothers were eliminated by underworld assassins.

His next objective was to eliminate Dr. Martin Luther King Jr., protest marches, riots, and the constant movement to be equal as the US Constitution stipulates.

J. Edgar Hoover hated the black race in general and always considered them as second-class citizens. He really did not consider them citizens at all. If the truth were known, I doubt that he wanted them guaranteed any constitutional rights at all. Therefore, this thorn in his side had to be eliminated. The Kennedy elimination worked; so why not use the underworld to do the job for him without bringing himself under suspicion?

First came the $50,000 reward, filtered to the underworld as only Hoover knew how to do. Now comes James Allen Smith—a two-time loser, ex-convict, a smart, intelligent con man, manipulator, who thought that the world was a sucker. A man who desired to start at the top. I have seen him sit in my rocker for hours at a time, smiling and talking to himself, planning a scheme to get something for nothing. He conned his mother and I out of thousands of dollars. He became a first-class hoodlum who wanted the world without working for it. I should know; he was my stepson.

He finally maneuvered himself into a corner and situation of no return. Hence, the final desperate move in March 1968 to finalize the partnership with Hoover to assassinate Dr. King by setting up and double-crossing James Earl Ray. He had already double-crossed his mother and I and his former crime boss. But the big boss was in charge at this point in time, so it was James Smith who was double-crossed by Hoover who let the underworld carry out yet another assassination for him. What goes around comes around.

Now comes James Earl Ray, a lifetime habitual criminal, a man with a cruel background. Misunderstood, mistreated, and neglected in his early years. He is a man who was brought up in the rough side of town where criminals congregate and whores abound. His lifestyle and background was seasoned bait for my stepson to exploit. This was the perfect man to set up, the man that Smith had longed to meet. Ray took its hook, line, and sinker and is now sitting in prison for life, scared to death for his future survival, in fear of saying or doing the wrong thing. By reading between the lines in his book, I could sense this. He never goes into detail about any of his meetings with Raoul. I am truly convinced that Ray did not shoot Dr. King. He was blocks away when the trigger was pulled, learning by radio while driving back to the scene of the shooting. Ray immediately left for Atlanta when he heard over the radio that the suspect assassin was driving a white Mustang.

In regard to my short, six-month friendship with Bud Fensterwald, I must write the following:

> He was a former attorney of James Earl Ray who tried in vain to get him a new trial. He founded the Assassination Archives and Research Center. This man had dedicated his life to get at the truth, not only in the death of Dr. King, but also in regard to the Kennedy assassinations. He was truly a great American citizen. He used his personal funds to start this organization. He had the grit and followed through, likened unto a bulldog and Winston Churchill. He was a humanitarian, a man of integrity, and was devoted to his endeavors, wherever it might take to get the job done.

Bud, your spirit and dedication has driven me to write this book, to finish where you left off.

May your soul rest in peace. God bless.

# CHAPTER 13

# The FBI Papers

The death of my wife and the unsolved murder of her son has only intensified the sense of duty that I feel toward continuing my investigation into the involvement of James Allen Smith in the death of Dr. Martin Luther King Jr. The diligent manner in which I pursue this investigation is hampered continuously by the way I am forced to carry on my investigation. At times, I feel as if my hands are tied.

I'll give you an example of what I am talking about. After Bud Fensterwald made a special plane trip to interview me regarding my investigations in the fall of 1990, he in turn intensified his own investigations.

The first thing that he did was to request that any and all papers held by the FBI concerning the matter be sent directly to him. This request was not frivolous or out of line in any way. This man was James Earl Ray's former attorney and president of the Assassination Archives. The total amount of material held by the FBI concerning this matter was known to be 624 pages of material. This request was made through the Freedom of Information Act in late December 1990. I have in my possession a copy of this request and a letter of refusal from the FBI. The letter of refusal was based on the grounds that it would be a violation of the Personal Privacy Act.

On August 1992, I requested the very same papers. One month later, I received 124 of the pages. Four hundred and eighteen pages were omitted. These pages were omitted on the same grounds that they were denied to Bud. All the papers released were that Smith was a suspect in connection with stealing and transporting of stolen cars from 1966 to midsummer of 1969. The papers contain a good physical description of James as well as documenting his background as a convicted criminal.

During this particular period of time, the FBI was always about six months behind Smith's activities. They did not know of the Caddy deal with the SCLC and Hosea Williams's connection with Smith. Bud was able to verify this by obtaining information about the arrest and release of Hosea Williams. Williams was released because of insufficient evidence.

Let's use some old-fashioned common sense here. Let's use that horse sense way of thinking that I spoke about at the beginning of this story. I asked for 624 pages of material on file with the FBI concerning James Allen Smith and his criminal activities that they monitored by their own admission. The FBI released material from 1966–'67 to me relating suspicions of car theft. I already knew that he was a car thief. The FBI would not release the other 418 pages that I requested. These 418 pages of information were not withheld from me because they contained something about James that I already knew. They contained information that I was not ever supposed to find out. This is not some brilliant conclusion on my part. It was the simple process of deduction.

Let me tell you about some of my deductions. No more car thefts were reported to the FBI from mid-July until Smith's demise. I am led to believe that the papers kept from me documented other activities. These activities probably include telephone calls from New Orleans as well as other forms of communication with the FBI. They could have included personal contact with the FBI as well as direct telephone communication with them. If there was any suspicions of car theft during this time, I would surely have received them through the requested papers. So I can only assume that there is an attempt at a possible government cover-up when such restrictions are placed on the availability of these and other documents that would shed some light on the truth in regard to this matter as a whole. The general public will always be held hostage to the truth concerning these kind of matters until the laws of the land are reversed on special cases such as this one. Such is the case in releasing the papers concerning the assassination of President Kennedy.

I would like to offer some personal comments as to the reasons why the FBI has not released all of the material on James Allen Smith to Ray's attorneys or to myself.

The FBI cannot release these papers. The papers would document the direct involvement of the FBI as the perpetrator in the assassination of Dr. Martin Luther King Jr. The FBI would be shown to have been working directly with James Allen Smith.

Kitty Anderson was James Allen Smith's ex-wife. Her association with my wife provided more information about James and the FBI. According to her, James was being issued a new ID card by the FBI and being sent to Argentina. Kitty Anderson believes to this day that James is alive in South America and will return some day. The body identified by autopsy in Austin was that of James Allen Smith. The coroner came to this conclusion despite the fact that the remains had lain in an open pasture from April until July of 1968.

These papers cannot be released because the last days of Smith would be revealed in complete detail. These details would include what happened immediately before and after the King assassination.

In summary, I feel that the missing pages indicated possible proof of a direct cover-up by our illustrious FBI. I have put in years of investigation. Not only do I want the truth to come out regarding the conspirators in the King assassination, but I also want to bring out the truth about who murdered my stepson. My stepson was James Allen Smith, alias Raoul.

One has to read the true story of the life James Allen Smith before you can identify him as being the same person James Earl Ray said he knew only as Raoul. This is that story. Why can't we see the other four hundred and some odd pages on James Allen Smith? What tale do they tell? What vital information do they hold? Why won't the FBI release files? I have no hopes of obtaining them. Both Jim Leser, president of the Assassination Archives in Washington, and I have filed appeals. The only response is an acknowledgment of an appeal stating that we would have to stand in line due to a backlog of previous appeals. This could take months or even years. In the meantime, we are left in limbo at the discretion of the FBI. The only thing left is for one to guess and wonder. I have my own guesses. What are yours?

So I will end by asking the same question, as did James Earl Ray: Who killed Martin Luther King Jr.?

If you feel that you have any information that would lead to the arrest and conviction of anyone involved in the assassination of Dr. Martin Luther King Jr., or any information that might affect the imprisonment of James Earl Ray for committing this crime, feel free to contact your local FBI office.

Actual correspondence letters between the author and both Bud Fensterwald and James H. Leser of the Assassination Archives and Research Center in Washington, D.C.

Raoul as a child

Raoul

James H. Lesar, President
918 F Street, N.W. • Suite 510
Washington, D.C. 20004
(202) 393-1917

October 6, 1992

Mr. Glen R. Tennis
P.O. Box 8
San Angelo, TX 76902

Dear Mr. Tennis:

At long last the FBI has released 124 pages (out of 542 pages) from its Headquarters file on James Allen Smith.  I am sending them to you under separate cover.

Please advise me of anything in these materials that you think is significant.

In order to protect your rights, I have lodged an appeal of the FBI's withholdings with the Office of Information and Privacy (the OIP), the Justice Department's appeals unit.  A copy of my letter to the OIP is enclosed.

Sincerely yours,

Jim Lesar
President, AARC

Letter requesting information from the FBI

*Washington, D.C. 20530*

September 16, 1992

Mr. Glen Tennis
Post Office Box 5856
San Angelo, TX   76902

    Re:   James Allen Smith

Dear Mr. Tennis:

This is to advise you that your administrative appeal from the action of the Federal Bureau of Investigation on your request for information from the files of the Department of Justice was received by this Office on September 14, 1992.

The Office of Information and Privacy, which has the responsibility of adjudicating such appeals, has a substantial backlog of pending appeals received prior to yours.  In an attempt to afford each appellant equal and impartial treatment, we have adopted a general practice of assigning appeals in the approximate order of receipt.  Your appeal has been assigned number 92-2401.  Please mention this number in any future correspondence to this Office regarding this matter.

We will notify you of the decision on your appeal as soon as we can.  The necessity of this delay is regretted and your continuing courtesy is appreciated.

                  Sincerely,

                  Drema A. Hanshaw
                  Paralegal Specialist
                  Office of Information and Privacy

Letter to request freedom of information – Raoul

James H. Lesar, President
918 F Street, N.W. • Suite 510
Washington, D.C. 20004
(202) 393-1917

July 6, 1992

Mr. Glen R. Tennis
P.O. Box 8
San Angelo, TX 76902

Dear Mr. Tennis:

Please accept my apologies for not having responded sooner to your letter to me of April 26, 1991.  Trying to run the AARC ("Assassiantion Archives and Research Center") and practice law at the same time is proving very difficult.

Thanks for sending me the news clipping quoting me.  Unfortunately, Congress is not going to release the records of the House Select Committee on Assassinations pertaining to Dr. King's murder at this time, just those pertaining to President Kennedy's assassination.

I don't have time to deal with James A. Smith at the moment. We'll just have to wait until the FBI finally gets around to releasing his file.  I'll let you know as soon as they do this.

Sincerely yours,

Jim Lesar
President, AARC

Letter to request freedom of information – Raoul

**U.S. Department of Justice**

Federal Bureau of Investigation

---

*Washington, D.C. 20535*

AUG 2 6 1992

Mr. Glen A. Tennis
Post Office Box 5856
San Angelo, TX   76982

Subject:   James Allen Smith
FOIPA No.  363,382

Dear Mr. Tennis:

Enclosed are copies of documents from FBI records. Excisions have been made to protect information exempt from disclosure pursuant to Title 5, United States Code, Sections 552, subsections b3, b7C, b7D and b7E.  Where excisions were made, the appropriate exempting subsections have been cited opposite the deletions.  See Form 4-694a, enclosed, for an explanation of these exemptions.

Exemption b3 has been used in conjunction with Rule (6)(e) of the Federal Rules of Criminal Procedure.

Pursuant to your request, 542 pages were reviewed and 124 pages are being released.

You will note that some material was deleted using the notations that the information pertained only to a third party with no reference to you or the subject of your request or that the information pertained to a third party with the name of the subject of your request listed only in the title.  These documents were scoped to ensure you did not have to pay a duplication fee for material that did not pertain to the subject of your request. Please be assured that all material pertinent to your request was processed for release.

If you desire, you may appeal any denials contained herein.  Appeals should be directed in writing to the Assistant Attorney General, Office of Policy Development (Attention: Office of Information and Privacy), United States Department of Justice,



Letter to investigator (page 1)

Mr. Glen A. Tennis


Washington, D.C. 20530, within thirty days from receipt of this letter.  The envelope and the letter should be clearly marked "Freedom of Information Appeal" or "Information Appeal".  Please cite the FOIPA number assigned to your request so that it may be easily identified.

Sincerely yours,

J. Kevin O'Brien

Chief
Freedom of Information-
    Privacy Acts Section
Information Management Division

Enclosures (2)

Letter to investigator (page 2)

BERNARD FENSTERWALD, JR.

Attorney at Law

SUITE 900, TWIN TOWERS BUILDING
1000 WILSON BOULEVARD
ARLINGTON, VIRGINIA 22209

(703) 276-9297

November 15, 1990

James Earl Ray, Inmate
State Penitentiary
P.O. Box 1000
Petros, Tenn. 37845

Dear Jimmy,

It has been a long time since we have been in touch. However, I have stumbled across some information which <u>may</u> repeat <u>may</u> help get you out of prison.

I wish to come to Petros to see you, but did not wish to make the trip if, for some unknown reason, you did not wish to see me.

Jim Lesar joins in best wishes.

Sincerely yours,

Bud Fensterwald

copy

Letter to James Earl Ray in prison for the
murder of Martin Luther King

ASSASSINATION ARCHIVES AND RESEARCH CENTER
918 F. ST., N.W.
WASHINGTON, D.C. 20004
(202) 393-1917

April 29, 1991

Mr. Glen R. Tennis
P.O. Box 5856
San Angelo, TX 76902

Dear Mr. Tennis:

Thank you very much for your letter of April 12th.

I am familiar with the story regarding your stepson, James Allen Smith. Bud Fensterwald went to Tennessee to visit James Earl Ray last and did relate your allegations to him and show him the picture of your stepson. Jimmy declined to make any identification. (Bud and I both represented Jimmy for several years. Like Bud, I believe that there was a conspiracy to assassinate Dr. King).

I am not presently able to come to Texas to see you. I am aware that Bud made a Freedom of Information Act request for FBI records on James Allen Smith several months ago. The FBI has indicated that it has about 400 pages on him. Unfortunately, the FBI is very slow in responding to Freedom of Information Act requests, so it will probably be at least several months before it releases these records. I will let you know as soon as we hear from them, and of course I will send a copy of everything they release.

Sincerely yours,

James H. Lesar

Jim Lessar letter to me (Glen R. Tennis)

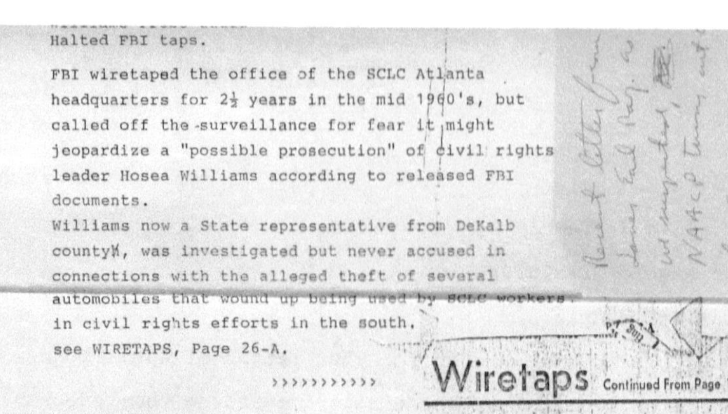

Halted FBI taps.

FBI wiretaped the office of the SCLC Atlanta
headquarters for 2½ years in the mid 1960's, but
called off the surveillance for fear it might
jeopardize a "possible prosecution" of civil rights
leader Hosea Williams according to released FBI
documents.
Williams now a State representative from DeKalb
countyM, was investigated but never accused in
connections with the alleged theft of several
automobiles that wound up being used by SCLC workers
in civil rights efforts in the south.

see WIRETAPS, Page 26-A.

>>>>>>>>>>>

## Wiretaps Continued From Page 1-A

## FBI-Black Activist Plan To Remove King Bared

WASHINGTON (UPI) — Newly released files reveal the FBI and an unidentified black activist worked together "in an effort to eliminate (Dr. Martin Luther) King" a few years before the civil rights leader was murdered.

The late FBI director J. Edgar Hoover's secret office files were obtained under a Freedom of Information Act request by the Center for National Security Studies, a private organization, and published yesterday.

The name of the collaborator was blanked out in the released document, which was dated Dec. 1, 1964.

"(Blank) stated to DeLoach (another top FBI official) that he was faced with the difficult problem of taking steps to remove King from the national picture," the memo said.

"HE INDICATES in his comments a lack of confidence that he, alone, could be successful. It is therefore suggested that consideration be given to the following course of action:

"That DeLoach have a further discussion with (Blank) and offer to be helpful in connection with the problem of removal of King from the national scene."

It suggested that (Blank), black leaders such as James Farmer and labor leader A. Philip Randolph, and "on a highly confidential basis could brief such a group on the security background of King" ... including "the use of a tape . . . with a transcript for convenience in following the tape, (and) should be most convincing."

THE SENATE Intelligence Committee reported in 1976 that the FBI had bugged hotel rooms used by King, allegedly recording meetings he had with women.

With the purpose of "destroying his marriage," the Senate report said, the FBI mailed King a copy of the recording, with an accompanying note "which Dr. King and his advisers interpreted as threatening to release the tape recording unless Dr. King committed suicide."

In another document made public Sunday, then-Atty. Gen. Nicholas Katzenbach gave Hoover blanket authority to carry out electronic surveillance in his absence without prior authority as was required at the time.

King was shot and killed in Memphis, April 4, 1968. James Earl Ray, an escaped convict, pleaded guilty to the murder and is serving a 99-year prison sentence.

Two other men, Harold Belton Andrews and Morris Finley, who is now an Atlanta city councilman, were convicted in connection with the alleged thefts. Finley was later allowed to enter a 'no contest plea and sentenced to two years probation.

The wiretapping of the SCLC's Atlanta office, the Atlanta residence of the late Dr. Martin Luther King Jr. and the New York office of the SCLC was described in a series of memoranda from the "official and confidential" files of the late FBI Director, J. Edgar Hoover.

The files were released after they were demanded by the Center for National Security Studies under the federal Freedom of Information Act.

According to one internal FBI memo, the wiretap was installed at SCLC's Auburn Avenue headquarters, Nov. 8, 1963, and "maintained" until June 21, 1966, "when Attorney General Nicholas Katzenbach ordered it discontinued since he thought it might be prejudicial to the possible prosecution of Hosea Williams, Southern Christian Leadership Conference official, under Interstate Transportation of Stolen Vehicles Statutes."

A number of documents in the 317-page file show that Williams' link to the case stemmed from a charge by another defendant in the case — apparently Andrews — that he had stolen cars to sell to the SCLC's voter education effort, which Williams headed. The documents indicate that to substantiate the reference ture of dated without bureau

dated June 22, 1966, said that because of the "ramifications" involving SCLC and the civil rights movement, the prosecution was being handled by the Justice Department's Washington-based criminal division rather than the U.S. attorney's office in Atlanta.

Williams said Tuesday the the two stolen cars that were used by SCLC workers were purchased in Atlanta, and he indicated they were virtually the only ones out of "30 or 40" that were not donated by a new-car dealer in Connecticut through the SCLC chapter there.

He said that at one point the allegations that he was implicated in the thefts were so strong and persistent that King personally called Williams into his office and asked whether he was involved.

"He said, 'I want you to tell me the truth, Hosea,' " Williams recalled. " 'As long as I believe in your character, I can fight for you . . . did you buy those cars knowing they were stolen.'

"I said, 'Dr. King, honest to God, I did not.'

"He said, 'I believe you; go on home. Rest in peace.' "

The FBI documents reveal that King's Atlanta home was under electronic surveillance from Nov. 8, 1963, to April 1965. Although the authorization for the wiretaps, signed by then-Attorney General Robert F. Kennedy, covered any residence to which King might move, the documents indicate that the surveillance was ended when he moved to a new home.

According to the documents, a total of 14 "bugs," or listening devices, and a tape were

By CHARLES HASSLETT
WASHINGTON —

Bernard Fensterwald; 12/31/90

Bernard: the story was interesting, particularly about the Dude stealing cars for the NAACP. AS can be noted above, the SCLC was reported to have been in the business.

So it would seem Smith's threat against MLK

James Early Ray's commitment to Bud Finsterwald

SUBJECT: James Allen Smith

FILE: 15-59658

FBI file on James Allen Smith

Glen R. Tennis

## Glen R. Tennis

Glen R. Tennis, formerly of Clayton, died Sunday, April 14, 1996 after an extended illness at San Angelo, Texas. He was 80.

Funeral services and burial were set at Lawnhaven Cemetery in San Angelo, for Wednesday, April 17.

Mr. Tennis was born at Kingfisher, Oklahoma August 16, 1915, the son of E. A. and Jeanette Tennis. He spent his early years in Clayton, graduating from Clayton High School with the class of 1933.

While here, he worked and helped run the Tennis Dairy.

He moved to San Angelo, where he was a livestock auctioneer for many years, and also had a furniture auction business.

He was preceded in death by his wife, Ethel, in 1986; and a brother, Bill Tennis; and a sister, Anna.

Survivors include three children, LaVern Minton and a son Johnny Tennis, both of Odessa, Texas, and an adopted son, Billy Tennis of San Angelo; several grandchildren; three sisters, Marjorie McLaughlin of Clayton, Laura McVean of Durango, Colorado, and Betty Haggerton of Wimberley, Texas.

Glen R. Tennis, obituary

BERNARD FENSTERWALD, JR.
Attorney at Law
SUITE 900, TWIN TOWERS BUILDING
1000 WILSON BOULEVARD
ARLINGTON, VIRGINIA 22209
(703) 276-9297

November 15, 1990

James Earl Ray, Inmate
State Penitentiary
P.O. Box 1000
Petros, Tenn. 37845

Dear Jimmy,

It has been a long time since we have been in touch. However, I have stumbled across some information which may repeat may help get you out of prison.

I wish to come to Petros to see you, but did not wish to make the trip if, for some unknown reason, you did not wish to see me.

Jim Lesar joins in best wishes.

Sincerely yours,

Bud Fensterwald

Bud reveals he believes Smith to be Raoul

**U.S. Department of Justice**

Federal Bureau of Investigation

*Washington, D.C. 20535*

MR BUD FENSTERWALD
ASSASSINATION ARCHIVES AND
　RESEARCH CENTER
918 F STREET, N.W.
WASHINGTON, D.C.　20004

FEB 2 6 1991

SUBJECT OF REQUEST: JAMES ALLEN
　　　　　　　　　　　　SMITH

FOIPA NO: __342880__

Dear MR FENSTERWALD:

　　　　This is in further response to your Freedom of Information/Privacy Acts (FOIPA) request(s). Information pertaining to your request has been set forth below in appropriate paragraphs.

☐ The additional data requested from you has been received.

☐ We have received your request which was referred from our ________________________ Office(s) to FBI Headquarters for handling.

☐ We are currently conducting a search of indices to our central records system files at FBI Headquarters to determine if we have the records you are seeking.　Upon completion of this review, we will advise you.

☐ We have located documents which may pertain to your request(s), and we will assign them for processing soon.

☒ We have received your letter expressing your willingness to pay fees of approximately __$30__ .

☐ We have received your check in the amount of ____________ , dated __________________ .

☒ The large number of FOIPA requests received by the FBI has caused delay in processing your request(s).　The FBI has allocated substantial resources, including manpower, to insure that delays in responding to FOIPA requests are minimized. We solicit your understanding and assure you that we will process your request(s) as soon as possible.

　　Your continued patience will be appreciated.

☐ See Continuation Page for additional information.

Sincerely yours,

*J. Kevin O'Rin.*

Chief
Freedom of Information-Privacy Acts Section
Records Management Division

Bud reveals he believes Smith to be Raoul

March 8, 1991


Mr. J. Kevin O'Brien, Chief
FOIA Section
Records Management Division
FBI
Washington, D.C.  20535                    FOIPA No. 342880


Dear Mr. O'Brien,

Please refer to your letter of February 26, 1991, a copy of which is enclosed for your ready reference.

We formally seek an exception to your Open America rule in this case under the theory of deprivation of liberty.  Please see attached a copy of page 1143 of 722 F.Supp. 1137 (S.D.N.Y. 1989) Ferguson v. FBI, in which the court holds: "Moreover, the court finds that plaintiff's liberty interests require expedition."

Although the Assassination Archives is the technical requester in 342880, the requester in interest is James Earl Ray, who is serving a life sentence in Tennessee for the murder of Dr. Martin Luther King.  A major reason for Ray's guilty plea was his inability to identify the mysterious "Raoul" who, he claims, organized the assassination.  Requester Assassination Archives has reason to believe that James Allen Smith (deceased) was "Raoul" and that the FBI's records relating to him might give grounds for re-opening that controversial case and possibly leading to a reduction in Ray's life sentence.

Might we point out that there are only 400 pages of documents in question, and that fees will be paid.

Bud reveals that he believes Smith to be Raoul, page 1

We ask you, as a matter of discretion, to make an exception to <u>Open</u>
<u>America</u> in this matter and process the records "out of order".


                              Sincerely yours,


                              Bernard Fensterwald, Jr.

                              President of AARC



Enclosure

BF:jan



cc: James Lesar
    Glen Tennis
    James Earl Ray

Bud reveals that he believes Smith to be Raoul, page 2

4-824 (Rev. 4-8-88)

**U.S. Department of Justice**

Federal Bureau of Investigation

*Washington, D.C. 20535*

MR BUD FENSTERWALD
ASSASSINATION ARCHIVES AND
  RESEARCH CENTER
918 F STREET, N.W.
WASHINGTON, D.C.  20004

FEB 26 1991

SUBJECT OF REQUEST: JAMES ALLEN
                      SMITH

FOIPA NO:  342880

Dear MR FENSTERWALD:

      This is in further response to your Freedom of Information/Privacy Acts (FOIPA) request(s). Information pertaining to your request has been set forth below in appropriate paragraphs.

☐ The additional data requested from you has been received.

☐ We have received your request which was referred from our _______________________
Office(s) to FBI Headquarters for handling.

☐ We are currently conducting a search of indices to our central records system files at FBI Headquarters to determine if we have the records you are seeking. Upon completion of this review, we will advise you.

☐ We have located documents which may pertain to your request(s), and we will assign them for processing soon.

☒ We have received your letter expressing your willingness to pay fees of approximately _$30_ .

☐ We have received your check in the amount of _____________ , dated _____________ .

☒ The large number of FOIPA requests received by the FBI has caused delay in processing your request(s). The FBI has allocated substantial resources, including manpower, to insure that delays in responding to FOIPA requests are minimized. We solicit your understanding and assure you that we will process your request(s) as soon as possible.

Your continued patience will be appreciated.

☐ See Continuation Page for additional information.

Sincerely yours,

J. Kevin O'Brien

Chief
Freedom of Information-Privacy Acts Section
Records Management Division

Bud reveals he believes Smith to be Raoul

4-744 (Rev. 8-27-86)

**U.S. Department of Justice**

Federal Bureau of Investigation

*Washington, D.C. 20535*

MR BUD FENSTERWALD
ASSASSINATION ARCHIVES AND
  RESEARCH CENTER
918 F STREET, N.W.
WASHINGTON, DC  20004

[JAN 0 2 1991

Request No. _______ 342880

RE: SMITH, JAMES ALLEN

Dear Requester:

☒ This acknowledges your recent Freedom of Information-Privacy Acts (FOIPA) request submitted to the FBI.

☐ Based on the limited information you provided, we cannot make an accurate search of our records. Please furnish your complete name, alias, date and place of birth, prior addresses, employments, and any specific data that would permit us to locate the documents you seek.

☐ Please submit your notarized signature. This procedure is designed to insure that documents, if located, are released only to an individual having right of access to the information.

☐ If you want a search of our Identification Division records for any arrest record that might pertain to you, please comply with the enclosed instructions set forth in Attorney General Order 556-73. Fingerprint impressions are needed for comparison with records in the Identification Division to insure that an individual's record is not disseminated to an unauthorized person.

☒ We are currently searching the indices to our central records system files at FBI Headquarters for any documents which may pertain to your request. Upon completion of this search you will be notified of the results.

☐ Provide the complete name, date and place of birth for the subject of your request. If subject is deceased, give date of death and any proof of death you have.

Your request has been assigned the number indicated above. Please use this number in all correspondence with us.

Sincerely yours,

J. Kevin O'Brien/SJ

Chief
Freedom of Information-
  Privacy Acts Section
Records Management Division

☐ Enclosure

Bud, investigator

# About the Author

Anthony Tennis lives in Florida, retired to a place by the lake. He works a little and he fishes. He enjoys feeding the birds and working in his garden. His cats are a great help as they chew all day. He grew up in West Texas as an only child. He moved to Florida in 1998. He is single and happy. Best Wishes to everyone reads this book and please keep it or give it to a friend as it will become forgotten history never revealed